GRIEVING DAD

GRIEVING DAD

SURVIVING AND HEALING THE LOSS OF YOUR CHILD

BY MARK SEIDMAN

ISBN: 1540879534
ISBN-13: 978-1540879530

DEDICATION

This book is dedicated to my son Eric Seidman. In his short time here, he lived life to the fullest. Even when he was very young, he loved to bring people together and he always looked for ways to help others to be their very best.

Eric made me proud in more ways that I can count. He looked for the good in everyone and he would go out of his way to help anyone, especially if they were going through a hard time. He was always eager to share what he had learned and he has inspired me to share what I've learned about healing the deepest of all emotional wounds.

A PERSONAL NOTE

My son was 26 when he died as the result of an accident.
While the specifics of your loss are different than mine,
I absolutely understand the horror of losing a child. During
the first year after Eric died, I learned how to endure the total
misery of my loss and how to begin to heal my broken heart.

I know that nothing I can say will take your pain away, but I
hope that the lessons I have learned will comfort you, inspire
you, and help you move forward to rebuild your life.

You can't choose the hand you're dealt.
But you can choose how you play it.

INTRODUCTION

This was not supposed to happen. But it did.

You don't need me to tell you that this is the worst thing that can happen to any dad. You already know this. You've been thrown into the worst nightmare of them all. Except this is no nightmare. It's real. And now you've got to figure out how to get through it.

When Eric died, I was totally devastated. I couldn't eat. I couldn't sleep. I could barely breathe. And I was scared. I worried that this huge hole in my heart would prevent me from ever being happy again.

I knew there was no going back to the life I had before, but I had no idea how I could ever be OK again after suffering this huge loss.

After a few weeks, I figured out what I needed in order to build some kind of normal life in the aftermath of this emotional torpedo: genuine understanding, credible hope and encouragement, and most importantly, guidance in finding my way out of the seemingly endless gloom.

I needed to talk with people who understood what I was going through. My friends and family did everything they could to comfort and support me, but in spite of all their best intentions, none of them had suffered this loss, so they couldn't really understand what I was going through.

I started looking for other dads who had lost their children, hoping that they might share what they did to get through this hell. I didn't have to look hard to find men who had been through this. I was surprised how many of us are out there.

Every dad I spoke with was sympathetic and knew the pain I was experiencing. Finding understanding turned out to be the easy part.

Hope and encouragement were a little harder to come by. Almost all the dads I spoke with understood my anguish, but some of them were every bit as lost as I was, even years later. This was kind of discouraging. Other men seemed to be doing OK, and while they often offered genuine words of encouragement, some of them followed that with disclaimers like "…but it's going to take years" or "…but it's going to be really hard." I knew they meant well, but I already knew this was going to be a long hard road. I wanted hope, not reminders of how hard it was going to be.

Fortunately, some of the men I spoke with did offer stronger words of encouragement. Whenever another dad gave me hope that I would eventually be OK again, I asked for any suggestions they might have for me. Most of these guys shared a great idea or two, for which I was very grateful.

But I was really hoping they'd say something like, "Here are the steps I took that helped me work thorough this." I knew that there wasn't going to be one universal formula for getting through a loss like this. I was just hoping to get a better understanding of how they did it, so I could put together my own gameplan. Unfortunately, it just wasn't going to be that simple.

My next step was to see if there were any books that provided guidance from the point of view of a dad like me. When I went searching, I found lots of books on grieving. Many were written by women, some of whom were moms who had lost their children. Others were written by men, but most were psychologists and other "experts" who had not personally experienced this unimaginable loss.

I did find one or two books by men who had lost children that chronicled their experiences, but I never found a book written by a dad for dads that outlined steps I could take to find my way out of the black hole of gloom that surrounded me.

About two months after Eric died, I was having a particularly rough day. I felt like I was cursed to be miserable for the rest of my life. It was in that moment when I asked myself a question that would become a huge turning point for me: "What would Eric want for me, now that he's gone?" I instantly knew the answer: He'd want me to heal. He would want me to do whatever it took to rebuild my life. And he'd want me to rediscover happiness.

In the months that followed, with Eric as my inspiration, I dedicated myself to getting through this with dignity and integrity, even while enduring the hardest days. I made a promise to Eric and to myself that I would do whatever it took to figure out how to live the rest of my life the way Eric would want me to.

This didn't mean that it was going to be easy. This didn't mean that I would be done crying and missing him terribly. What it did mean is that I had clarity on my goal: I was going to honor Eric by getting through this. I knew right then that I'd somehow survive this and beyond that, I'd keep my promise to him to find my way forward to a life with all those things that had been ripped away from me when he died: comfort, trust, peace, fun, excitement, and passion.

And then I took it one step farther. I made a second promise to myself: If I could figure out how to be anything close to OK again, I would share what I had learned.

It's now a year since Eric died. It has been an extraordinary journey and I have learned a lot over the course of this year. I jotted down my first thoughts the day after Eric died, and every time something helped me, I made a note of it.

As the year progressed, I compiled and organized everything that I had learned. I wasn't sure what format would be best, but over time it became clear that the best thing to do was to develop it into the book that would have helped me navigate my way through this ordeal.

I hope that my experiences and the lessons I have learned will comfort you, inspire you, and help you to find your way from despair to hope to actually being OK, even happy again.

I don't know where you will be in your process when you get this book. You may be in the first week, or it might be months later. I'm going to do my best to make this relevant to you no matter how long it's been since you lost your child.

I want you to know one thing for sure: It's going to get better. While we can't get our kids back, we can find our way back to being OK again.

Here are the things that helped me…

THE BEGINNING

You get the news and your life is shattered. There are no words that can adequately describe the initial impact of learning that your child has died, but shattered comes close. In the beginning, everything feels bleak. All you feel is despair. And you have every right to. Life as you know it is over. Nothing will ever be the same again.

I know you know this. I wrote it because I wanted you to know that I, and the other unfortunate dads like us, have endured this too. But here's the good news: While the first phase is horrible, it doesn't stay this bad forever.

A loss this big destroys your plans, and as much as you want to get back to your feet, you may have no emotional strength or balance. Your emotional equilibrium may be shot. It's pointless to fight it. All you can do is breathe and put one foot in front of the other.

The beginning is awful. Your main goal is to survive it. There's not really much more you can do. In the weeks immediately after Eric died, I felt so incredibly lost and disoriented.

What I didn't know then and what you might not know now, is that there are things that can help you, even in the first few weeks. Some of them helped me take big steps forward.

I don't know that there is a perfect word to describe the things I've learned. In this book, I'll call them "guideposts." As you go forward, I hope you'll find that these guideposts will help you. Some will help more than others. The ones that are the most helpful for one dad may mean less to other dads. But looking back on my first year, I'm confident that many of these will help you move forward.

Here's the first guidepost:

Guidepost #1 – You can't plan, organize, prioritize and schedule your grieving. We discussed this in the introduction, but it bears repeating. These tools, which are so effective for so many things, are virtually useless when it comes to grieving. This was a big revelation for me. A big part of my success at work and in life came from "planning my work and working my plan."

You have to let go of control. This was very hard for me and it may be hard for you too. But the first phase of grieving the death of a child is like being on a raft on a very wild river. You go where it takes you. It's all you can do just to hold on as the huge rapids whip you every which way. You can't see around the next bend in the river to anticipate what's next, but it will eventually settle down and become more tranquil. There will be a time for you to take back control of your life. Just not yet.

It's natural to try to take control when your world is spinning out of control, and if you try to do this, it's just going to make it harder. Instead, you need to trust that your thoughts and feelings will settle down over time. Because they will.

Guidepost #2 – Everyone grieves differently, so your grieving process will be unique. There is a wide spectrum of ways that people process their grief. There is no one right way to do it. Some people find their way to accepting the loss sooner than others. No way is better or worse, just different. Keep that in mind as you confront your own grief and as you encounter others in their grief. Just as you can't plan your grief, you can't anticipate how anyone else is going to handle theirs either.

Similarly, no one else can tell you how to grieve. It's a very personal process.

Getting this hideous news can put you in shock at first. You may find yourself numb. But your loss is real and your feelings will come.

Guidepost #3 – Feel what you feel. If you're sad, let yourself be sad. If you're angry, let yourself be angry. It's a whole new world now. For a while, intense feelings will hit you from out of nowhere. Or you'll see something that reminds you of your child and you're instantly thrown into an emotional state. Don't fight it.

I'll make this next point bluntly: Feeling like crap feels like crap. Feeling despair and sorrow is a miserable experience, so it's understandable that you might want to avoid these feelings. That's a big mistake. Stuffing these feelings won't work. The feelings will find their way out one way or another and fighting to hold them in can even make you sick.

But here's the good news. If you allow yourself to let your bad feelings out, they will pass. No matter how sad I was and no matter how hard I cried, the despair faded. It's like throwing up. It's awful when you experience it, but it eventually passes and you feel better getting it out of your system.

You'll go through these miserable times over and over at first. That's necessary to getting past this first phase of grieving. Over time, your toughest times will become less severe. But make no mistake about it; you've got to let your feelings out to begin really moving forward.

Guidepost #4 – Don't hold back your feelings and don't shut down. When intense feelings hit you, it's important to express them, especially in the beginning. So, cry, scream, hit things, collapse, yell, get hysterical. It doesn't matter what anyone else thinks. The force of this is too strong to fight. So cuss, yell, pound the floor if that's how you feel. People may try to soothe you, but that's not what you need in the beginning. In the beginning, you need to allow yourself to have a full visceral reaction. Don't fight your feelings and don't hold back. You just lost your child. Nobody is going to judge you in any way. Everyone knows that you've suffered the most terrible loss, so no one is going to think less of you if you let your emotions out.

Guidepost #5 – After you let your feelings flow, calm yourself. While it's important to feel your genuine feelings and express them, this can sometimes cause you to feel like things are worse than they are. Feelings can build and build to the point that you mistakenly conclude that your life is ruined.

So while it's important to feel and express your feelings, it's also beneficial to know how to settle yourself down when you are at your saddest.

If you find yourself very distressed, here's one way to calm yourself: Breathe. Slowly. Sit or lie down, whichever is more comfortable for you. Breathe in through your nose and out through your mouth a few times. Keep that going and focus on the top of your head and relax just that one part of you. Then, work your way down your body slowly, relaxing your cheeks, your neck, your shoulders, chest, arms, etc. As you do this, your emotions will soon settle down. It may take a few minutes. You'll still be sad, but when you're calm, you're much less likely to feel like your own life is destroyed. It's not about denying your loss. It's about helping yourself begin to accept what must be accepted.

Guidepost #6 – Lots of people may reach out to you, and many have no clue what to say or do. At first, lots of people will want to support you and console you. People will have all kinds of reactions and many of them will be awkward because no one knows how to react to a loss like this. Just as you are dealing with something very rare, so are they.

Some will just hug you and say nothing, because the truth is there just aren't words that will console you.

Some people will say kind and supportive things.

And some people won't know what to say or what to do, so they'll sometimes say or ask things that seem insensitive or even stupid. When this happens, try to accept their feeble efforts with as much grace as you can muster. Remember that they mean well.

And finally, some may say they understand. Unless they've lost a child of their own, no, they don't understand. But they also mean well.

FOUR THINGS
YOU NEED TO KNOW
RIGHT NOW

Every time a father loses a child, the circumstances are unique. Your life is different from mine. Your child was different from mine. You loss is different from mine.

But while the details of your loss are not the same as mine, you and I do have one terrible thing in common: Our child is gone. Whether it was sudden or the end of an illness, it's the worst nightmare imaginable. It happened to me and now it has happened to you. You're now a member of the club that no one wants to belong to.

And while our circumstances are different in some ways, here are four things I can tell you with confidence:

1) Your life will never be the same, but…
2) You're going to be OK
3) It's going to take a while, and…
4) It will be very rough at first

The first days are unbearable. Impossibly hard. But even as early as one week after Eric died, I started to see the first rays of hope. In the beginning, they didn't last long. Maybe only a few seconds. But as time went by, I slowly started to feel hopeful and optimistic more and more.

This is a long, hard journey, but it has a destination. Your life will never be exactly as it was but you ultimately want to find your way to a life with happiness and optimism. Having that destination as your goal is important because you can't find your way if you don't know where you're trying to go.

Right now, you may only be feeling gloom and sadness, but after a while, there will be light at the end of the tunnel. As time goes by, you will work your way toward a productive and fulfilling life.

I know it's a huge blow. I speak from experience: It's the worst thing that will ever happen to you and it's absolutely hideous. But you have to take it head on. You can't deflect it and you can't dodge it. It's impossibly hard at first, but it does start to get easier over time. Let's go back to those four statements:

1) Your life will never be the same, but...
2) You're going to be OK
3) It's going to take a while, and...
4) It will be very rough at first

We'll take them one at a time. Let's get the two hardest ones out of the way first.

It's going to take a while.

The "it," of course, is your healing. You need to understand that whatever your path forward is, it's going to take some time for you to heal and move forward. This loss is bigger than any other, so it's easy to understand that it's going to take longer for this to heal than it might take for other emotional wounds. You'll notice that I deliberately didn't specify any timetable for your recovery. That's because everyone's experience is unique. I really don't know how long it will take you to recover from this. No one does. But what we can do is focus on ways to make the process smoother and shorter. So while there are specific actions you can take, there just can't be a timetable on this.

You may or may not be a patient person under normal circumstances, but impatience won't serve you now. Although this may seem counter-intuitive, the sooner you accept that you have to be patient, the sooner you'll get through this.

I am not a patient person by nature, so I fought this at first. I tried to set timetables and milestones for my emotional recovery. Big mistake, especially in the beginning. You can influence how fast you regain your life's equilibrium, but you just can't set a timetable for your journey back to OK-ness.

This part is going to be hard on some guys. A lot of us are dialed into schedules, objectives, and plans and we tend to apply a timetable to most processes. But you can't impose a timetable on your healing.

What we can do, is focus on actions we can take to help us move forward. And the good news is that there are several specific things you can do that will help you through this ordeal. But there's no escaping the fact that it's going to take a while to heal.

It will be very rough at first.

At first glance, this may seem negative, but it's actually good news. When you look closely at the statement "It will be very rough at first" you realize that what it actually means is that it won't always be as rough as it is in the beginning

It will get better.

This is very important and you need to really think about this for a bit. No matter where you are in your process, you can be virtually certain that it will get better as time goes by. If you're really miserable, you may need to take this on faith at first. You may not see any way out of your despair… yet.

It doesn't really matter whether you believe this is true, but you absolutely will get better over time. It may not feel like this applies to you, but it does. It applies to everyone. Even with this horrible loss, we are all wired to heal and move forward from emotional trauma.

It's vitally important you remember this, even if you find it hard to believe at this moment. You will start to heal and you will move forward. It's in your DNA. You can't help it.

I didn't think I'd ever feel happy again, or excited, or playful, or feel any strong positive emotions. But over time, I started to experience all these things again. And so will you.

So yes, it will be rough at first. But it won't stay that bad. You will feel better and better over time. Remember, you can't set a time goal and you can't rush it. But it is going to happen.

Your life will never be the same.

Just like the last one, this one sounds worse than it really is. This is because you are looking at it through a very gloomy lens right now. You've been thrown into a tailspin, so it's easy to understand that you might be very, very negative right now.

But as your hurt begins to fade, there will very likely be some unanticipated, positive by-products that come from this loss. It's not uncommon for new friendships to form and old ones to be rekindled. So while your life has changed forever, that doesn't mean that your life is ruined. Not at all. Yes, you've suffered a massive loss and yes, your life has been forever altered. But when the dust eventually settles, there will be some positive by-products of your loss. You might become motivated to make some positive changes in your life. Or you might be inspired to do something to honor your child's legacy.

And most importantly:

You're going to be OK.

You probably can't believe that right now. It may not seem possible. But it's true. Yes, it will take a while. Yes, it will be rough at first. Yes, your life will be changed. But the most important thing for you to know, even though you may be suffering terribly right now, is that you absolutely will eventually be OK. And although you may not be able to imagine it now, you'll be on your path to being OK sooner than you think.

FINDING STRENGTH WHEN YOU HAVE NONE

Guidepost #7 – Take care of yourself. It may be hard to focus on taking care of yourself, but it's vital that you do. You've just taken a huge blow and you're severely weakened. You need to rebuild your strength and the only way to do that is to take care of yourself. You may not want to focus on yourself right now, but there are some important reasons to do so.

1) You are under a lot of stress. If you don't take care of yourself, you can get sick. That's the last thing you need right now.
2) Others may be counting on you. You may have a wife and/or other children who are relying on you to help them. More on that shortly.

Here are the basics of taking care of yourself:

- Eat (part 1) – You won't want to at first, but you've got to get nourishment. Even if you have no appetite, eat small portions of healthy food.
- Eat (part 2) – Allow yourself to have some of your favorite treats. In addition to eating healthy food for nourishment, I also ate quite a bit of mint chocolate chip ice cream. This small indulgence was actually my first very small oasis in my desert of gloom.
- Get some exercise – Don't just sit around or lie in bed all day. You don't need to do your full workout but you do need to move a little bit. Even walking around your

house a little bit is better for your psyche than sitting and lying around all day.

- You need to sleep – While I don't normally like taking medications, I made an exception during this extraordinarily stressful time. Consider asking your doctor for sleeping medication if you can't sleep.
- Keep up on basic grooming – Take showers, wash up, brush your teeth and shave (if you did before). When you're down, it's easy to let these things slide. You don't have to get all dressed up, but don't hang out in your PJs or your dumpiest clothes.
- Find people you can talk to honestly about how you feel and tell them how you're doing, no matter how bad it is.
- Accept every hug that comes your way, even from people you barely know and even if you really weren't much of a hugger before.
- Play your favorite music (but not the sad songs... You're sad enough already).
- Tell the people at work that you're going to need some time and you're not sure how long it will be. They'll understand.

Guidepost #8 – Let your friends and family help you.
When disaster strikes, people tend to go to one extreme or the other. They either become immobilized, unable to do what needs to be done, or they try to do it all themselves.

Neither of these is going to work very well. If you ask others to handle everything, you'll feel bad about it later. And if you try to do it all yourself, you'll be overwhelmed. So step up and do what needs to be done, <u>and</u> recruit people you trust to help you. And believe me, they will. People desperately want to help, but they have no idea what to do. And to make matters worse, they generally won't do anything unless you ask. Not because they don't want to help, but because they are afraid that they'll do something to upset you.

So when you ask someone to do something for you, they will almost always be very eager to help. If you need food, ask for it. If you need help with preparing for a memorial service, ask for it. If you need someone to talk to, ask for it. Almost everyone will be happy to know that they've helped you out in some way. If ever you can be confident of people rising to the occasion for you, this is it.

Guidepost #9 – Accept that you might be a zombie for a while. Even as you take care of yourself and let others support you, after the initial shock settles down, you may find yourself in a transitional phase where you aren't in the intense despair of the first phase, but you aren't anywhere near feeling anything that resembles normal. You may find that you just can't connect with people. Going out, even just to the market, can seem very weird. Your memory may not be good at all. Your feelings may be all over the place, numb one minute, sad the next, then disoriented.

While this phase isn't as intensely miserable as the beginning, it just doesn't feel good at all. It can be very frustrating. If you find yourself in this state, try to remember that it will pass. Your mind is working hard to make sense of your previously unimaginable world. And this is another important part of the long road back to being OK. Try to be patient. Like the first phase, this phase will pass.

Guidepost #10 – Be honest with yourself about the support you need and get it. You need what you need, and this is not the time to deny what you need. You may not like needing what you need, but more than any other time, this is the time to be honest with yourself and get the support you need.

It's very possible that other people will have strong opinions on the kind of support you should seek. None of that matters. The only thing that matters is whatever it is that will help you through this difficult time. If you don't have clarity on the kind of support that will be most helpful, you can certainly "test drive" different types of support until you find what feels best for you.

There is lots of support available to you. What you have to do is find the support that fits you best. Here are some examples you may want to consider:

- Support Groups for parents who have lost children: For example, there is a group called Compassionate Friends (www.CompassionateFriends.org).

- You can seek out other dads who have lost children. There aren't a lot of us, but we're out there. If you start asking your friends if they know of anyone else who has lost a child, it probably won't take long until you find someone.

What you have to keep in mind is that everyone you speak to will have their own perspective and their own advice. Be selective about who you include on your support team. There's a very simple litmus test: Ask yourself this question after you speak with anyone: "Is this person helping me move forward on my path to healing?" If yes, you have a very good reason to continue with them. But if not, politely move on.

Guidepost #11 – Consider working with a therapist.

If there was ever a legitimate reason to get a therapist, this is it. The death of a child is the most stressful event that one can experience. And just about any therapist can help you through the most difficult parts of this. The decision to seek out a therapist is your and yours alone, but it's worth considering, even if you elect not to pursue that path at this time. If things stay bumpy down the road, you can always revisit that decision.

Guidepost #12 – Consider meeting with your clergy.
Your relationship with God, your religion, and your place of worship is very personal. It's not my place to tell you that "you need to go to church." But meeting with a spiritual leader can be very helpful. Here's why:

Every religion that I'm aware of has something to comfort those who are grieving. Every member of the clergy has helped members of their congregation through the unbearable sadness of the loss of loved ones. And if they've been spiritual leaders for a while, they have probably helped others who have lost their children. Even if you're not "a regular," they'll welcome you with open arms. And they'll do everything they can to help you heal your wounded soul.

Guidepost #13 – Understand that most of those people who showed up in the first few days will soon disappear.
It would sure be nice if everyone got together and spread out their visits and support, but it doesn't work that way. Just as it is with the more common case of losing a grandparent or parent, you hear from almost everyone in the very beginning and then they leave and get on with their lives. Even with this extraordinary loss, it will be pretty much the same. Don't let yourself be disappointed when this happens. As you're working hard to build your strength, that last thing you need is to get caught off guard asking yourself, "Where'd everybody go?"

It's perfectly normal for most people who aren't in your inner circle, to stop to pay their respects and then resume their normal lives. But your good friends and close family members will almost certainly continue to be supportive after everyone else has paid their respects.

YOUR TWO IMPOSSIBLE TASKS

In the first weeks, everything is hard. Some things are really hard. And some things just seem impossible.

In reality, there is very little that you absolutely must do. If you just aren't up to it, everyone will understand. For example, you don't have to take visitors if you're not ready.

I clearly remember how hard everything was in my first few weeks. But knew that I needed to dig down deep and somehow rise to the occasion to take on two immensely difficult tasks.

If you can muster whatever strength you have to do these two seemingly impossible tasks now, you'll be very thankful later. I fully realize that this may be too much to ask right now and no one will think less of you if you just can't do this.

But if you can dig down deep and take on these two tasks, you'll know in your heart that you did the right thing when it mattered most. You'll never regret it and the road ahead will be easier.

Guidepost #14 – Take good care of your close family. You've just absorbed the biggest shot a man can take, and you may be so devastated that you can barely do anything, let alone help anyone else. But you're not the only one impacted. Your immediate family will be looking to you to help them through their grief too. You're all in this together so you don't need to be the only one in the caretaker role. But if you can take the lead and set the tone, you can make it just a bit easier for everyone.

As soon as possible, get your immediate family together and let everyone know that we're all in this together and we'll all get through it together. Remind them of Guidepost #2 (Everyone grieves differently). Let them know that you're there for them. Remind them that we all need to take care of each other. And to be especially compassionate and gentle with one another right now.

Hearing this from you when their worlds are crumbling will mean a lot. And hopefully, you'll get some love and care back.

Even if you don't believe it yet, continue to remind your close family that "we'll get through this" and "we'll be OK." From time to time, just give them a hug without any words. Ask what you can do for them.

In addition to helping them, there is a huge secondary benefit from taking care of others, even as you're in pain yourself: The act of caring for others will make you feel a little bit better (and maybe more than just a little bit). I realized this when I gave reassurance to my wife and daughter. When I helped them, I almost always noticed that I felt just a bit better.

Guidepost #15 – Do what needs to be done, and do it the right way, no matter how hard it is. There will be a number of things that need to be done, and many of these tasks will seem unbearably difficult. Dig down deep and do the best you can to handle these tasks in the way that best honors your child and his or her legacy. If you handle all these things with dignity and respect, even when it seems impossible, you will never regret it.

Even if you abdicated some of this earlier, you can start right now to do what needs to be done and do it in a way that will make you proud later. If you haven't made arrangements for memorial services, start now. This starts the process of honoring your child's legacy, which we'll discuss in more detail later.

The last thing you want is to look back and regret how you handled things during this time. But if you do what needs to be done with as much honor and dignity as you possibly can, not only will you avoid looking back with regret, you will heal faster knowing that in your darkest hour, you honored your child by handling things the right way. While this is an immensely huge challenge, it will help you heal faster and move forward with your life.

MY FIRST MAJOR TURNING POINT

This section is about one of my personal experiences. While the details are specific to me and my son, this concept is very powerful and it can work just as well for you.

After you get past the first weeks in which every day is miserable, you'll start to find that some days are better than others. On one of my tougher days about six weeks after Eric died, I was deep in my sadness, searching for something to help me move forward. I was seriously stuck in my gloom. And then, out of nowhere, this amazing idea came to me:

What if Eric could be granted one minute to come back and give me guidance? He was young and he died suddenly and unexpectedly, so there was never a reason for us to discuss this while he was alive. We both expected that I'd go first in the normal way. And then he was gone.

But what if he actually could come back for that one minute to let me know what he really wanted for me now that he was gone? As soon as that thought occurred to me, my mind raced to come up with the answer. Lots of thoughts swirled around, so I knew that I was going to have to live with this for a while in order for his truth to settle in.

I knew him very well. I'd seen him react to all kinds of things, good and bad. Although he was just 26, he had started to acquire some wisdom and it was his wisdom that I wanted to access. (Even younger children have a very special clarity and wisdom, so even if your child was younger, this concept can still work just as well for you.)

I really didn't know what would come of this, but I forced myself to sit still and think about it. I wrote about what he might say in a moment of complete candor. Over the course of several days, a few things kept coming back every time I thought about this. As I had hoped, when it all settled, there were just a few specific thoughts I was virtually sure he'd share with me if he were to be granted exactly 60 seconds to share them:

- At first be devastated. We loved each other so much. We were so important to one another. If I died suddenly, he'd be devastated too. So of course he'd expect me to be crushed in the beginning. He'd want me to grieve thoroughly and not hold back.

- But he wouldn't want me to spend the rest of my life grieving. Under no circumstances would he want me to be stuck in an endless vortex of grief. In fact, I'm sure he'd be unsettled and maybe even angry if he somehow knew that I was forever locked in a state of grief.

- He'd absolutely want me to find my way back to living my life with happiness, excitement, passion and peace. Although he was gone, leaving a void that could never be filled, he wouldn't want his death to take the life out of me. It would be a long hard road but we often talked about not shying away from the hard stuff.

- And he'd want me to think of him every day. But he'd want more than just that: About 90% of the time, he'd want me to remember him in a good way. Once in a while he'd want me to miss him. But way more often than that, he'd want me to think about our great times together and how proud he made me.

And then his minute was over. I could certainly check off the first point about grieving hard. The second and third points about not getting stuck and finding my way to living a good life became my compass, pointing the way forward.

I knew that last point was going to be the most challenging. I do think of him every day. And I'm sure I always will. But I knew it would be a while before I could honestly say that I'd be happy 90% of the time when I thought of him. Like all of this, it would be a process. But knowing that's what he would want, I knew that sooner or later, I'd get there.

Right then and there I made it my mission to heal and live the way I knew he'd want me to. I knew it would take time and I knew it wouldn't be easy, but now my goal was clear and my motivation was strong: I was going do what I knew Eric would want me to do: I was going to get through this somehow and heal my broken heart. He made me so proud of him. Now it was my mission to make him proud of me.

Guidepost #16 – No matter how young your child was, spend some time to ponder what they would want for you now that they're gone. I believe that they want some kind of good for you. And when you get clarity on this, you can begin to turn in a new and better direction.

A special note to dads who may have had a difficult relationship with their child: If your child died while there was significant conflict between you, it's best to do a variation of this exercise. Think of your child when they were at their best, even if you hadn't seen that side of them for a while. Every one of us has a best side, even if some haven't shown it for some time. So, even if you were in the midst of challenging conflicts at the time your child died, he or she still had a best side and it is that part of them that wants the best for you.

One evening, weeks later, I was having another tough time, struggling with my sadness. Even though I was very down, I still had clarity on three things:

1) I believed I deserve to heal and move forward.
2) I wanted to heal and move forward.
3) Eric would want me to heal and move forward.

And yet, there I was, sitting in my office chair, stuck in my sadness, seeing no way forward. And then an idea came to me that helped me immensely. I don't know where it came from. It just popped into my head. It was a very clear visualization of the Grand Canyon.

I was standing at one rim, looking across to the other side. And I was taken by how far away the other side was. And how deep the canyon was. And how steep the sides of the canyon were. As I gazed across, I knew that life was good on the other side. Somehow, I was certain that I was going to get there. But there were two things I didn't know: I didn't have a clue as to how I was going to get there, and I didn't have any idea about how long it would take.

Having this visualization was a very weird experience. It was vividly clear and yet those two unknowns were so vague. It was a little bit comforting that I believed I'd get there. I knew that meant I was going to somehow be OK. Over the next several weeks, the image kept coming back to me. Each time, I thought about how I might be able to get to the other side, but it took a few weeks before the answer came.

I started to think of ways that one might get across a canyon. You could scale the wall to get down to the bottom, cross the river somehow, and then figure out a way to climb to the top of the other side. Or you could ride a mule down, across and up. Since I knew this was some kind of a metaphor, I didn't limit my options to practical ways. Maybe I was supposed to be shot across from a giant circus canyon. Maybe a helicopter would fly me across. Or maybe a magic carpet. None of these seemed to resonate as my true way to get across.

And one day, it hit me:

Miners often built wires across (much smaller) canyons and then they'd go across in a small cart. To get to the other side, they'd have to pull themselves across. It was a lot of work and it took a lot of time if the canyon was wide, but it was an effective way to get across a treacherous canyon.

And I knew that this was my way across. The metaphor was perfect. Rebuilding my life would be a lot of work. It would not be fast. And then there was the wind. On some days, there would be no wind. I'd move forward as much as I could pull myself forward. But sometimes there would be a headwind. And if the headwind was weak, I'd have to work just to maintain my position. So there were going to be some days where I made no progress at all no matter what I tried. If the headwind was strong, it might even push me back in spite of all my efforts to move forward. So no matter what I did, on some days I was going to slip backwards.

But sometimes there would be tailwinds. The wind would help move me forward, even if I did little or no work at all. And if the wind was at my back when I was working hard to get to the other side, I'd make big progress toward healing and going forward with my life.

And this is exactly how it has been. As time goes by, I'm slowly healing and I'm gradually making progress toward finding my way back to a fulfilling life. I take it day by day. Some days, I move forward just a little bit and some days I just kind of hold my own. Once in a while, I seem to go backwards. And some days I feel like I'm making real progress.

But every day, I work on it. Every day, I pull myself forward. I can't control how the wind affects me, but I know that if I just keep pulling myself forward, I'm going to get there.

My minute with Eric and my visualization about the Grand Canyon gave me something I desperately needed: Hope.

And no matter how awful you may feel right now, there's hope for you too.

STARTING TO MOVE FORWARD

Moving forward is impossible at first. But over time, you will be able to restore normalcy in your day to day life. If this seems inconceivable right now, that's OK. You're just not there yet. But you will be.

Guidepost #17 – You will slowly emerge from being a zombie. When Eric died, my cognitive skills were very weak. I started to worry that the emotional trauma I had suffered was so severe that it did some kind of permanent damage to my ability to think clearly. But my mind did become sharp again and, while it may take weeks or months, yours will too. Your memory will function as it did before. And you'll start to get your energy back. I can't tell you how long it will take. It's a gradual process. I'm sure it's different for everyone, but I want to assure you that you will eventually be every bit as sharp as you were before.

Guidepost #18 – A powerful way to help yourself. This one may not be easy, but it is very powerful if you stick with it. Right now, decide that you're going to do whatever it takes to find your way to happiness. Note that I didn't say "…find your way <u>back</u> to happiness." We can never go back to what we had. But we can find happiness again.

The concept of being happy again may seem completely ludicrous right now. That's totally fine. The key is to assertively declare that you will find your way to happiness. Though it may seem like a complete leap of faith, making this affirmation starts (or accelerates) the process of moving forward.

So starting right now, choose to be determined to heal. Even if you don't believe it's possible. Just decide right this minute that in spite of everything, you are going to heal. Say this out loud, "I am finding my way to being happy again." I know. It's absurd. So do it in private. But say it with conviction. Start telling people, "I don't know how long it will take, but I am going to heal and move forward."

This is an exercise in perseverance. It may feel wrong, uncomfortable and insincere at first. But in actuality, it's true. You may not know how long it will take, and you can count on setbacks, but if you remind yourself every day that you're going to heal and you're going to find your way to happiness, you absolutely will.

Guidepost #19 – You'll probably need to initiate your prior social connections. No one really knows when and how to re-engage with you in a normal way. They want to give you plenty of space to grieve, so when you're ready to begin reconnecting with people, you'll probably need to be the one to initiate it. You may have to give yourself a nudge to re-enter your social life, but don't wait until you're all the way ready. The time to reach out is when you feel like you're starting to get ready.

People want to hear from you. More than anything, they want to know that you're on a path to being OK. No one will expect you to be all the way OK, but just to know that you're getting a bit better day by day. Once you break the ice with this opener, things will get much easier. Ask them how they've been. They'll be happy to update you. They may ask if you want to get together. Say yes. It doesn't matter what you do, just do anything that you would normally do with them. This is an important part of your healing process. And you'll almost certainly have a good time.

Guidepost #20 – You've got to talk about it honestly.
After the initial shock subsides, barricading yourself emotionally just prolongs your agony and may jeopardize your health. The biggest mistake you can make is to try to suck it up and plow forward. Starting with your most trusted friends, talk honestly about your loss and what you're feeling. It may be hard at first, but it's very cathartic and no one is going to judge you. While it may be hard at first, talking candidly with your most trusted friends about how you're really doing, helps you make progress on the path to a better emotional state.

This doesn't mean that you talk about your child non-stop to anyone and everyone. But you need to talk about this to help you get to the place where you can begin to accept the reality of your loss. Think about all the people in your life.

Who are you most comfortable being yourself with? Or who do you have in your life that you can call 24/7? Or who do you trust to listen to you and not judge you? If you haven't done so already, make a short list and call one of these people as soon as you can. Tell them you'd like to spend some time with them to decompress. (Use whatever word you feel comfortable with to describe this.)

If you don't have anyone in your life like this, you can always go to any member of the clergy, even if you don't belong to their religion or attend at their place of worship.

No matter who you choose to speak with, find a place where you can speak in private. If you're not sure what you're going to say, don't worry about it. You can think about what you might say on the ride over, but don't be surprised if what you end up talking about is very different than you thought it would be.

When you get together, sit down, relax and just start talking. Start by telling the person that you just want to talk about what's going on. You don't need them to do anything but listen. They don't need to advise you or have any wisdom. What you need is a safe place to just talk about it. They'll understand. You'll be amazed how much you'll get out. You may cry. You may laugh. You may rant. Just let it out. All of it. Honestly. Don't censor yourself.

The other person may have a suggestion or they may just acknowledge what they hear you saying. But mostly they should just let you talk. You'll be amazed how much better you feel when you do this.

Guidepost #21 – Be ready for all the "first time since" encounters. At first, everyone is there and then they go back to their everyday lives. Your family and closest friends will probably continue to support you and check in on you, but most people will give you space. As you resume your regular routines, you will run into people who you have seen since the very first days and others who you haven't seen at all since your loss.

"First time since" encounters are a great example of the expression about "the elephant in the room." Everyone knows it's there, but no one knows how to talk about it. Sometimes, they will ask how you're doing. Other times, they'll just feel a sudden burst of sadness. After all, seeing you is an instant reminder of what happened.

"First time since" encounters can be uncomfortable for you and for them. But if you have a couple of prepared responses like "I'm taking it one day at a time," you'll get past those first awkward moments.

The good news is that once you get past this first encounter, subsequent encounters are much easier.

Guidepost #22 – You may have very low tolerance for other people's problems. As you start to get back up on your feet, people will start to interact with you in regular ways. This is a sure sign of progress. And once in a while, someone is going to gripe about something. It's very possible that this might really irritate you.

I remember the first time this happened to me. I was slowly getting back into my old routines and I ran into a friend. He started complaining about some issue at his work. All of a sudden, I was really bugged by this. I wanted to yell, "I don't want to hear about your piddly little problem. You want to know what a real problem is? I'll tell you what a real problem is! My son died two months ago. Do you still want to complain about your little problem?" Of course, I didn't say that or anything like that. But I realized that I was very sensitive about hearing people gripe about their problems.

Once I realized that this was a hot button for me, I just kind of tuned out when other people complained about this or that. And with a little bit of practice, this didn't bug me nearly as much. Other guys have had similar experiences, so keep a lookout for this. If you're aware that you might be sensitive to this, it won't be as bad if someone shares a gripe.

Guidepost #23 – When to go back to work. As with all of this, there isn't a precise timetable for returning to work. Some people are ready in a couple weeks. Others need much longer. No one can tell you when you're ready, but if you're honest with yourself, you'll know when the time is right.

Don't use your loss as a way to avoid a job you don't like, but don't go back too soon either. Immersing yourself in your work can be therapeutic, but it shouldn't be a way to avoid your feelings or trying to compress your grieving into a shorter period. So go back when you're ready to go back.

Guidepost #24 – How to go back to work. Once you've made the decision to return, let the company know a few days before your date of return. You will never get more support and tolerance than you will now, so don't hesitate to be honest about whatever you need to make your return to work as smooth as possible for you.

If you have a Human Resources department, use it. They should be very supportive and they should be your advocates now, more than ever.

If you have a boss, be honest with him or her about what you need and any concerns you may have about returning to work.

If you supervise a team, meet with them ASAP to let them know that you're OK (even if that's only partly true) and to get back up to speed.

You're going to have to endure being looked at. It's not fun to be "that poor guy" but at first, that's who you're going to be. Your coworkers won't know how to handle it. They don't want to say or do the wrong thing, so they are likely to avoid you. Your best bet is to be proactive and take the lead. Find opportunities to re-engage with people on normal business stuff as soon as you can.

If you're part of a small team, see if you can round everyone up for a quick impromptu meeting to break the ice. It can be as simple as this: "I want to thank everyone for picking up the slack while I was gone. It's been a tough month, but I'm glad to be back. Don't be surprised if I drop a ball from time to time. Just let me know if I let anything fall through the cracks. If anyone needs to go over anything with me, you know where to find me. I've got a bunch of things to catch up on but I wanted to thank you again for all your support." (Start to head back to your desk.) There may be some nice response like "We're glad you're back." Acknowledge them and get to work. When people see you back in your normal work mode, they'll fall right back into their normal routines with you.

Guidepost #25 – Remind yourself of the good things you still have and be grateful for them. This is a key element in getting past the most intense phases of your grieving process. It's easy for your mind to gravitate toward the sadness of your loss, and it's unlikely that you're going to feel good about life until you start deliberately reminding yourself of all the good things in your life.

Get a piece of paper and make a list of people you still have in your life and great things/opportunities you still have in your life. Then start envisioning a few happy moments that may lie ahead with these people or things or opportunities. Don't get discouraged if it takes a few tries to get going on this. It's hard at first. But while you have suffered a huge loss, the other indisputable fact is that you still have all the other good things that you had before. And while your grief will eventually begin to fade, the goodness in your life will remain and grow. But when you're in a place of immense sadness, you need to retrain your mind to seek happiness.

Every night before you go to bed, write down five things you have to be thankful for. During the day, be mindful to stop from time to time to remind yourself what you have to be grateful for. Eventually, this becomes automatic, just like any other habit. This won't eliminate your sadness. But it will shift your sadness out of the foreground for a while.

THE THIRD IMPOSSIBLE TASK:

DEALING WITH YOUR CHILD'S ROOM

Dealing with your child's room and their things is one of the hardest things you'll ever have to do. But as with the other two impossible tasks, if you can dig deep to find the strength to handle this in a way that honors your child's memory, it will help you heal.

There are two obvious variations to this:

1) What to do with your child's room if your child lived in your home and
2) What to do when your child has moved away from your home.

The next two guideposts go together and apply in both cases.

Guidepost #26a – You'll never be 100% ready to deal with your child's things, so do this as soon as you feel you can.

Guidepost #26b – When in real doubt, hang onto it, but don't use this as a reason to keep more than you should.

Our story illustrates both.

In our case, our son had moved out. I'll discuss how we dealt with clearing out Eric's home and then discuss the additional challenges you'll face if your child lived in your home.

Eric's home was a seven hour drive from our house, so getting there wasn't just a simple matter of jumping in the car and running over there. And because his roommates were eventually going to need to rent his room to someone else, we had to deal with this sooner than we would have preferred to.

When my wife and I went to his home to clear out his things, I said two words to her: "Buckle up." I knew this was going to be tough and this was my way of reminding her to steel herself. I knew it would be hard. Boy was I right.

It wasn't going to be a simple matter of going in, grabbing his stuff, and heading home. Before we began, I determined that everything had to be divided up into five groups:

1) Things my wife and I would take (some to later be given to others)
2) Things Eric's girlfriend would take
3) Things his best friend/roommate would keep
4) Things that would be donated to charities
5) Things that would be thrown out

Going into his house was hard, but going into his room was just hideous. Because Eric died suddenly, his room was in a normal state of disarray, just as it would be on any morning when he left for work, expecting to come home at the end of the day.

He was an avid rock climber, so he had a lot of climbing and camping gear. He loved clothes, so he had a full closet and dresser. He had a wide range of interests from car repair to photography, so he had all kinds of stuff.

It took a full day. It was me, my wife, Eric's girlfriend, and his best friend. Every one of us needed every bit of support from the others.

If you've already cleared out your child's things, you know how hard it was. If you've avoided doing this, or if you've only partially dealt with it, do it as soon as you feel you can.

Whenever you choose to do this, be sure that you have someone there to give you moral support. You'll want this to be someone you can talk to when you can't decide what to do with a certain item. And you'll definitely want someone to talk to as the memories start bubbling up.

You don't have to resolve what to do with every item, but you at least need to go through everything and decide what to keep, what to give to others, what you're sure you will donate, and what you're sure you can throw away. When in doubt, keep it. But if you find yourself keeping items just because they belonged to your child, you'll keep everything. Part of moving forward is recognizing that some things need to go. For example, it's hard to imagine why you'd need to hang onto their socks, unless a certain pair of socks had specific sentimental value.

Donate what you're going to donate as soon as possible. Throw away what needs to be thrown away as soon as you can. It's hard. It can feel like disposing of part of your child, but it's not that at all. Your child lives on within you and keeping certain items helps you stay close to them. But disposing of items with no specific sentimental value can help you heal and move forward.

IF YOUR CHILD LIVED IN YOUR HOME

Your child's room in your home is now a sacred place. When you go in there, everywhere you look, you see your child. It's almost impossible not to break down and cry when you go into your child's room. Go there. Be there. Feel it all. It's awful, but it's also cathartic. It will slowly get easier, but it will never get easy.

And yet, you're going to need to deal with your child's clothes, their toys, their furniture and their décor at some point.

While there is no universal right way to deal with your child's room, it is important to work closely with the family members who live in your home to decide when the time is right for you and for them and how to go about it. And there is no universal right time. Once again, every situation is unique and everyone grieves differently.

To help everyone's emotional healing, sooner is better than later, but there is definitely a period that is too soon. Give your family a little time before taking this on. While you'll never be 100% ready to do this, you'll need to do it at some point. But don't start in on this if you feel it will be devastating for anyone who lives in your home.

It's easy to understand how you might want to leave your child's room exactly as it is as a kind of "shrine" to your child, but at some point it will be best for everyone to transform the room in some way.

When you are ready to begin, the first phase is to deal with their clothes, toys, and other possessions. This doesn't have to be done all at once, but doing it in bits and pieces over an extended period of time can be harder on your emotions than doing it in one or two sessions.

Guidepost #27 – Determine the next purpose of their room before you start removing their décor. The next phase is evolving the décor in the room. Since there are no external factors driving your timetable, take some time to decide what the next purpose of that room will be. If you have two other children sharing a room, perhaps it can become a room for one of them. Or maybe a guest room. Or an office. It's usually best to make this decision as a family team so that there is no resentment about what is done with the room.

While there is no specific timetable for changing the décor in your child's room, it's easy to get stuck and find reasons to leave everything as is. But as hard as it may be to transform their room, it's an important step on your path to healing.

Once you've determined the next function of the room, it's best to get going on it as soon as you can. It will not honor them or serve you to maintain their room as a perpetual shrine. While it's not easy taking down the wallpaper with bunnies or airplanes, once it's done, it's done. And once you've redecorated, you'll be another big step forward on your path moving forward.

A few years after Eric moved out of our home, I had converted his bedroom into an office. Even when he was alive, I kept a few things as they were as a reminder that this was his room. For example, I had put little glow in the dark stars on the ceiling. They are still there. After Eric died, I added a few of his things to the décor in the room. The room is clearly my office, but I like seeing reminders of Eric around the room.

HONORING THEIR LEGACY

Once you start to get your feet back on the ground, one of the best things you can do is find ways to honor your child's legacy. The truth we must all contend with is that there isn't a whole lot we can do for them now that they're gone. But one thing you can do is find ways to preserve their memory and help others gain inspiration from them.

How you honor their legacy is very personal. Every child is unique and every parent's relationship with their child is unique. Here are some possibilities:

You can ask that people make donations in your child's memory to any cause that may have meaning for you and/or your child. Even if your child was very young, this can be very fitting. If, for example, your child loved puppies, you can ask that donations be made to an animal shelter or other organizations that provide care for animals.

Some people set up small scholarships in their child's name. There are lots of ways to do this. Every high school will gladly help you facilitate this. It can be as little as $100.

You can plant trees in your child's memory. If you work with your local community on this, you can probably get them to agree to include a small plaque to commemorate your child. How you honor your child's memory is up to you. If you think about it for a while, I'm sure you'll come up with something that will feel right.

Very early on, I knew I was going to honor Eric's legacy. But it took a while before I started to figure out how.

Using tools that anyone can easily learn, I put together a website about him to share with anyone who knew him. The kids he went to college with may have known one side of him, but they may not have known other things that made him special. His cousins may have known some things about him, but they didn't really know other aspects of him.

But my strongest motivator was that his eventual nieces and/or nephews would never know their Uncle Eric. That really bothered me, so when the site was finished, I felt better knowing that they could at least learn about this wonderful guy that they'd never meet.

If you want to see an example of a website dedicated to a person who died too young, please feel free to check out the site. It's at http://markseidm.wixsite.com/eric. I hope you'll take a few moments to go through it. I think you'll find Eric to be a very inspirational guy.

Guidepost #28 – Find ways to honor their legacy. Give it some thought. Brainstorm with your closest family and friends. It may take weeks or months before you figure this out, but you'll know when something is right for you.

CONTINUING TOWARD YOUR NEW NORMAL

Ten years ago, I nearly died. I went in for what was supposed to be a simple surgical procedure. There was a complication and suddenly my life was in jeopardy. After a very long emergency procedure to save me, I woke up in an ICU with about ten doctors standing around my bed. I had no idea what had occurred, but I knew something wasn't right.

The doctors explained my situation and one of them said something that I'll never forget: He said, "You're not out of the woods yet." In that moment, my whole world was thrown off course. I faced a very long and difficult recovery.

I learned one very important lesson from this experience: It's in our DNA to heal. This applies to our bodies and our emotions. Sometimes healing can take a long time, but we are programmed to heal.

After a long and arduous recovery and rehabilitation, I am left with a very large scar going right across my gut that will be with me forever. I've accepted the fact that my body will never be the same as it was before. Over the last 10 years, my scar has faded somewhat, but it will never go away entirely.

The metaphor is easy to see. After Eric died, there came a point when I realized that I'd somehow be OK again. I'd have an emotional scar that would slowly fade, but it will never go away entirely.

We're all working to heal our deep emotional wounds from losing our children. We can and will get past the crushing agony of the first weeks, but we will all have to learn to live with our emotional scars. Working toward a more normal life comes with ups and downs. It took me a while to realize that my bad days were just that: bad days, but not a return to the seemingly permanent gloom of the first weeks. I eventually came to learn that bad days would pass and I'd get back to having better days very soon.

At first, it's impossible to imagine ever being happy again. And then one day, you find yourself feeling good about something, if even for just a minute or two. At some point, you'll have a good hour. And eventually a good day. As you move forward, this will start to happen more and more. This is a sure sign that you are healing.

Guidepost #29 – Moving forward is inevitable, but it isn't smooth. After some time has passed, you will probably find that in general, this week is a little bit better than last week. And next week will probably be better than this week. But this is not steady and it's not consistent. Sometimes you'll hit a plateau where you feel stuck and worse yet, there will be setbacks that throw you back to where you were earlier. All of this is absolutely normal. Sometimes it's "three steps forward, one step back." Other times it's three steps forward, four steps back." Wherever you are in your process, you will move forward.

You may feel like you're stuck sometimes, but that will be temporary.

You will move forward. But it won't be smooth. Knowing this in advance will help you minimize the discouragement when you inevitably slip back for a while.

Guidepost #30 – Anticipate challenging days. You'll have them, but they won't be as bad if you see them coming and prepare for them. Challenging days fall roughly into two categories: Those you can see coming and those that hit you out of nowhere. You have a pretty good idea what's coming up on the calendar. These days may not be easy, but at least you can see them approaching. As for the tough days that you can't identify on the horizon, just knowing that there will be some unexpected tough days will reduce the impact when they suddenly show up. Throughout my career, one of my recurring themes was "get ahead of it." Readying yourself for challenging days is a perfect example of getting ahead of it.

Guidepost #31 – Holidays, birthdays, and anniversaries will be challenging the first time through the calendar, but they will get easier over time. Don't let calendar events sneak up on you. You can see holidays coming so you have the opportunity to plan to make the best of them. The best example I can give you is how I handled my first Father's Day after Eric died.

Father's Day was less than three months after Eric died and I was dreading my first Father's Day without him.

I wanted to be sure that I planned the best possible weekend for myself while still honoring the guy whose birth made me a father in the first place. I scheduled a number of events for the weekend. Not at a frantic pace, but a steady stream of visits all weekend long. For me, the highlight of that weekend was a dinner at my son's favorite restaurant. My wife and daughter were there along with Eric's girlfriend. I told everyone that I wanted this to be a happy dinner. We drank a toast to Eric and shared some of our funniest stories about him. It wasn't all about Eric. We talked about all kinds of stuff as we might have under normal circumstances. We laughed a lot. The people nearby couldn't possibly have any idea that we had suffered this huge loss not even three months prior.

The next day, we visited my 92 year old dad, and once again it was a happy gathering. Of course, Eric was part of the conversation, but overall it was a happy visit with good food and lively conversation.

Every holiday, birthday or anniversary is an opportunity to remember good times. And it is absolutely appropriate to have a toast or some other tribute to your child who isn't able to be there. There will probably be a few tears mixed in, but with a little planning, holidays don't have to be miserable.

Guidepost #32 – Plan for your child's birthday and the anniversary of their death. This is one area where I have little to suggest. This is so personal that no one can tell you what to do. Here is what I can say: As with all holidays, don't let these events sneak up on you. Plan something. What you choose is entirely up to you. You may need to think about it for a while. It could be big or small. It might involve others or not.

However you choose to commemorate these days, your guiding principle is to honor your child's memory and their legacy. There is no right or wrong way to do this. Don't let anyone else tell you specific things you should or should not do. You can certainly ask for input if you want it, but the ultimate decision regarding how you honor your child on these days is up to you.

What you choose to do may be different every year. Or you may have a little ritual that you decide to do every year. This is one of those cases where your intuition will be your best guide.

There will be sadness on these days. It's honest and it's real. Be a little selfish and don't hesitate to ask for what you need. But when you focus on honoring your child's memory in whatever way is authentic for you, these days will be as good as they can possibly be.

Guidepost #33 – Don't be surprised when you get caught by surprise. Aftershocks can occur anytime. It happened to me. Several months had gone by. I had worked hard on healing and accepting Eric's loss. But then I read about another kid who had died and it just spun me. It was almost as if all the hard work I had done to get back on my feet was negated. Everything was bleak again.

What made it so hard was that it caught me by surprise. I had been doing so much better. I was starting to get back into my regular routines and enjoy my pastimes. And then all of a sudden it hit me. I just didn't see it coming.

I wish I had known this could happen. It took me a few days to rebound and get back to where I had been before. I don't think it would have been so bad if I had had some kind of a heads-up that this could happen.

Sad feelings can hit you from out of nowhere. That comes with the territory. This can be really frustrating and it can be scary. Don't let frustration or fear make it worse. Just let it flow through you. It will pass.

You need to walk a fine line with this. You don't want to be so sure it's going to happen that you more or less "invite" the sad feelings back. But at the same time, you don't want to get caught by surprise when something triggers sad feelings.

Guidepost #34 – Be aware of things that trigger sadness.
I found that, even after he was gone, some pictures of Eric made me smile, but others just broke my heart all over again. Some things reminded me of great times that we shared and other things just reminded me that his life was tragically short.

Eric died in a rock climbing accident. I had a picture of him working his way up a ridge with all his gear and a huge smile. But after he died, this picture just made my cry every time I looked at it. I knew I had to take that picture down.

This is an extreme and obvious example, but the same principle can apply to you. You'll always remember your child fondly, but if there are certain things that consistently make you sad, I'd suggest that you put these away, at least for a while. You can always revisit them months or years later, but while you're working to heal, these items can make the process of healing harder.

Guidepost #35 – Be aware of things that trigger good feelings. Hopefully, you have lots of happy memories of great times with your child and hopefully he or she gave you a lot to be proud of. After you get through the first hard months, you'll want to see things that bring back great memories.

Of course, this isn't black and white. It's more like, "most of the time I look at this, I have happy memories."

I started taking Eric fishing when he was about four and we worked our way up to fishing for huge tuna in the waters off of Mexico. On one of Eric's last trips, he caught a huge fish, way bigger than any I had ever caught. I have a picture of him with his 189 pound monster. The smile on his face reminds me of what a great time we had. Almost every time I look at it, I love the memories that it brings back. My office has a number of Eric mementos that bring back happy memories.

It took me a while to figure out which pictures and things tended to trigger happy memories and feelings and which tended to make me sad. But eventually, I started to realize which were which. Obviously, you need to consider the feelings of the others who live in your home, but to the extent you can, surround yourself with some pictures and items that bring the good feelings and put away the things that trigger sadness.

Of course on my occasional bad day, everything makes me sad, but after the sad wave passes, the pictures and things that made me smile before, make me smile again.

Guidepost #36 – Feel good when you feel good. As time goes by, you're going to find yourself feeling happy about this or that. This is normal and healthy, so enjoy whatever it is that brings good feelings your way. Celebrate happy events and triumphs. While your life isn't the same as before, good things still happen and good feelings follow along.

One of the biggest mistakes you can make is to shut down your good feelings when they come. I've talked to guys that felt guilty when they felt good. While this is easy to understand, it just doesn't serve you. Even with the weight of losing your child, there will still be happy moments and things to celebrate.

As I said earlier, allow yourself to feel whatever you feel. When you're sad, be sad. One thing I know for sure: You've had more than your share of sadness. So when you feel good, don't shut that down. When you're happy, just be happy. And you can take that one step farther. Look for people, things and situations that make you happy and enjoy them to the fullest.

WHEN I KNEW I WAS GOING TO BE OK

One day, several months after Eric died, I realized that I had hit a major milestone in my healing. Now looking back, it's clear that this was a culmination of doing all the things I had learned so far.

Shortly after Eric died, I had envisioned what he would want for me now that he was gone. (See page 39.) Knowing Eric as well as I did, I was certain that he wanted me to think of him every day with most of those thoughts being happy memories of him.

From time to time, I'd have a happy memory about Eric, but this would usually be followed by feeling sad again as the happy memory turned into a reminder of what I had lost.

One day I was telling someone about a funny moment from a time when Eric and I were fishing. He had been catching many more fish than me. Suddenly, he hooked another one and teased me mercilessly about it. Just as he was really rubbing it in, he lost the fish. We both saw the irony in it and had a big laugh about it.

As I was finishing the story, I realized that I was happy to be thinking about Eric and talking about him. There was no denying the joy of recalling this memory. And this time, it didn't turn into sadness as it would have before. This was an important breakthrough. It was the first time that I could be genuinely happy when talking about Eric.

As more time passed, this happened more and more often. I found myself talking about wonderful times that we had spent together. I found myself telling people about how proud I was of him for some of his accomplishments. More and more, I realized that I really enjoyed talking about him again. This came with a huge additional benefit. I had gotten to the point where I liked keeping his memory close to me. I didn't need to avoid him to avoid feeling sad.

Of course I miss him terribly sometimes. Of course I still have sad moments wishing he could be here for this or that. But mostly I like it when he pops into my head now. And I like talking about him. He was gone much too soon, but no one can take my happy memories of the time we spent together.

When I realized that I could once again keep him close in my thoughts without being overwhelmed by my sadness (at least most of the time) and enjoy talking about him (at least most of the time), I knew I was on my way to being OK.

When it dawned on me that thinking about Eric was once again a source of pride and wonderful memories for me rather than a reminder of my loss (at least most of the time), I knew I was going to be OK.

Guidepost #37 – After some time has passed, you'll enjoy sharing happy memories again. This might be the hardest one to believe, especially if you're in your first few months. It's going to take a while to get there, and it's going to take a lot of work on recovering from this, but there will come a time when you will be comfortable talking about your son or daughter.

YOUR NEW NORMAL

Guidepost #38 – You'll probably never be 100% done with grieving, but can still get on with your life. Much has been written about the five stages of grieving: denial, anger, bargaining, depression, and acceptance. It's very important for us to realize that acceptance doesn't come *after* the grieving is over. Acceptance is part of the grieving process.

Accepting the reality of your loss doesn't mean you're done grieving. What it does mean is that you are better able to rebuild your life. You'll return to work. You'll re-engage with your friends. You'll resume your routines and you'll get back into your hobbies and interests. You'll have your emotional scar, but that scar won't define who you are.

If you're still in your first few months, I know this must seem impossible to even consider.

Guidepost #39 – You'll be OK, but you'll need to keep working on it. Even as I have come to accept my reality and even as the routines of normal day-to-day life have pretty much returned for me, life has never been the same as it was before. I've come to accept that the emotional scar that I'll have with me forever means that I need to work just a little harder than most people to keep myself on a good path.

Here is a metaphor I use to describe this:

It's as if I'm in a kayak on a very slow moving river and I'm facing upstream. If I don't do anything, the current will slowly take me downstream to a darker sadder place. But if I paddle gently, with very little effort I can hold my own and stay right where I am. And if I use a bit more effort I can move slowly, but steadily upstream in a happier direction. And when I paddle harder, I can go faster and move decisively to an even better place farther upstream.

I find that most of the time, I'm OK doing that nice slow, steady paddling to maintain where I am or keep myself moving forward bit by bit. Sometimes, I paddle harder to strengthen myself and to be strong enough to help my wife and others. And once in a while, I just get too tired to paddle and drift back into sadness. But then I paddle hard to get myself back to being OK and resume the gentle paddling to stay there. I never drift all the way back into total despair. I always paddle forward before it gets that bad.

When I was describing my first few weeks I used the metaphor of huge rapids on a very fast moving river. It was as if I was on a raft using all my strength just to hold on as the river took me on a fast and terrifying ride. I couldn't control where the river took me. I could only hold on and hope that I'd survive the ordeal.

Compare that to the description of now being on a very slow moving river. And now I have a paddle. When you get past your first months, you'll start to realize that you have a paddle too. You'll be able to paddle upstream with just a little effort.

Once you're past the worst of it, most of what you need to do is take good care of yourself. For me, "taking care of myself" means a number of things. It can mean remembering to be grateful for all the good things I still have in my life. It can mean reaching out to someone I like and trust, and asking them to go to lunch with me. It can mean watching one of my favorite funny movies.

It's different for everyone, but even when we're having a rough day, deep down, we all know two or three things that will lift our spirits.

I've heard some people say that their entire life was ruined after the death of their child. I also heard people say that they really had nothing to look forward to or live for after the death of their child. This is how many of us feel in the first weeks after losing our child, but over time, you can find your way to your new normal, with strong relationships and many more good days than bad ones.

We need to remind ourselves that everything else that was good before is still good. Losing a child is hideous, but it doesn't have to destroy the other good things in our lives.

Guidepost #40 – There is no lemonade, but there are silver linings. You may have heard the saying, "When life gives you lemons, make lemonade." That's just fine for lots of things, but the inference is that you turn something bad into something good. It just doesn't work that way when you lose your child. Nothing can ever make this good. BUT, there is another saying that does apply: "Every cloud has a silver lining." While our loss never really goes away, there can, and probably will be some very powerful silver linings. Here are some examples:

In the aftermath of losing Eric, I have reconnected with a number of people who I was close to in the past. It's been great to have those people back in my life.

I look at my own life differently now. I am forever reminded that every day I get is an opportunity to do something meaningful. I don't take anything for granted any more. In spite of (and because of) losing Eric, I appreciate all the good things in my life more than ever. It may take you a while to get to this place, but once you've had a chance to work through the intense impact of your loss, and get back on your feet, I strongly doubt that you'll ever take anything for granted again.

The silver linings extend far beyond me and my family. I can't tell you how many people have told me that Eric's passing serves as a reminder to live their life to the fullest.

Here's one example:

A good friend of mine has a niece who went to high school with Eric. He sat down with her and a few of her friends to discuss how their lives were impacted by Eric's death. After talking about it for a while, the girls came away with one very clear message: There are no guarantees of a long and healthy life, so make every day count. They shared a round of hugs and the girls got up to go. He stopped them as they were about to walk out the door. He added three last words before they left: Don't get cheated.

TWO MORE THINGS THAT HELPED ME

Here are two additional things that helped me in the first months. The details are my personal experiences, but I hope you'll also benefit from each of them.

THE ROCK

One of our toughest days was the day we had to clean out Eric's things from the house he rented with two of his friends. As I discussed earlier, it took us a full day to go through everything, and it was a gut wrenching experience.

Knowing that we'd be physically and emotionally exhausted when we were done, I made reservations at a restaurant for that night so that we could have a nice relaxing dinner with Eric's closest friends. There would be eight of us. I selected one of Eric's favorite restaurants. It was a Lebanese place that featured round tables for eight. Each table had its own small fire pit in the middle.

We all met at the restaurant and found our way to our table. Our server lit our fire and our evening began. In contrast to our extremely difficult day, this dinner was wonderful. Everyone shared happy stories about Eric. We all laughed and smiled and hugged all through the four course dinner. The evening was everything I had hoped for and more.

The fire pit at the table is basically a bunch of very small rocks with a fire in the middle. To keep everyone safe, the fire is about two feet away from everyone, but the rocks extend much closer to the people at the table. Toward the end of the evening, I did something I ordinarily would never do: I subtly reached to the edge of the rocks and took one. I slipped it into my pocket. I wanted a souvenir from this extraordinary evening and now I had it.

I didn't think much about it after that. I just left it in my pocket with my wallet and keys and that's where it stayed until we got home the following evening.

After our seven hour ride home, we unpacked our car and settled down to relax before heading to bed. I took my wallet and keys out of my pocket and out came my little rock. For the first time, I took a close look at it. It was about ½ inch long by ¼ inch wide and tall, about the size of a kidney bean. I noticed that my little souvenir rock had two very distinct cracks in it.

My curiosity got the better of me and I decided to break the rock along one of the cracks to see what it looked like inside. I should add here that I've played guitar for years, and I have strong hands. I gave it a good effort, but the rock did not break. I'll also add that I'm a very determined person. So I wasn't about to give up. I picked it up again and gave it everything I had. I was sure that one of the cracks would give way and I'd see what was inside.

To my astonishment, the rock didn't break. The cracks were deep. It should have broken pretty easily, but it didn't break, no matter how hard I tried.

I held it in my hand and looked at it again. And that's when it struck me: This little rock was a perfect metaphor for me. On one hand, it had deep scars and it would have them forever. But on the other hand it was unbelievably strong, staying intact under a lot of pressure. Deeply scarred but impossibly strong.

That little rock sits on a shelf on my desk as a constant reminder that even though my emotional scars are deep, just like that rock, I remain very strong. I hope you'll come to see yourself the same way.

You can't manufacture experiences like this, but you absolutely can be open to things like this: ideas, metaphors, anything that can help you move forward toward a place of acceptance.

HENRY HOLLAND'S EULOGY FOR KING EDWARD VII

One day, my wife and I were heading home from visiting some friends. As I was driving, we both received an email from a close friend. I asked her to read it to me. In the email, he wrote that when his mother died, someone had sent him a written passage that helped him.

It turns out that this is very well known. It's possible that you may have seen it by now. It was written by Henry Holland, Canon of St. Paul's cathedral in London. He read it at the funeral of King Edward VII in May, 1910.

Here is what he said:

Death is nothing at all. It does not count.
I have only slipped away into the next room.
Nothing has happened.

Everything remains exactly as it was.
I am I, and you are you, and the old life that we lived so fondly
together is untouched, unchanged.
Whatever we were to each other, that we are still.

Call me by the old familiar name.
Speak of me in the easy way which you always used.
Put no difference into your tone.
Wear no forced air of solemnity or sorrow.

Laugh as we always laughed at the little jokes that we enjoyed
together. Play, smile, think of me, pray for me.
Let my name be ever the household word that it always was.
Let it be spoken without an effort, without the ghost of a
shadow upon it.

Life means all that it ever meant. It is the same as it ever was.

There is absolute and unbroken continuity.
What is this death but a negligible accident?

Why should I be out of mind because I am out of sight?
I am but waiting for you, for an interval, somewhere very near,
just round the corner.

All is well. Nothing is hurt; nothing is lost. One brief moment
and all will be as it was before. How we shall laugh at the
trouble of parting when we meet again!

As she got to the end of it, I was amazed. Three lines in particular stuck out for me:

"I have only slipped away into the next room."

"Whatever we were to each other, that we are still."

And finally…

I am but waiting for you, for an interval, somewhere very near,
just round the corner. All is well.

I needed that. I loved the positive spirit of it. And I loved how it reconciled accepting such a huge loss. While it's impossible to make sense of the loss of a child, I knew that if I could eventually embrace this way of viewing Eric's death, there was hope that I could someday be OK.

CLOSING THOUGHTS

Although it may seem inconceivable right now, after some time has passed, you will be OK. Since everyone is unique and the circumstances of your child's death are unique, it's impossible to predict how long it will take. But with a commitment to honor your child and heal your broken heart, you'll get there.

Your loss is front and center right now. You may be thoroughly consumed by it. That's totally appropriate and completely understandable. Getting back up on your feet, dusting yourself off, and starting to move forward is a long, hard process. I hope that some of the lessons I learned will help you as you move forward and heal.

Things will never be the same, but you can move forward into a new life that will include the interests and passions that you had before. And new ones. I took up kayaking. It's great therapy. Somewhere down the line, you'll also enjoy new things. Don't force it, but do be open to it.

I can almost guarantee that you'll think about your child every day for the rest of your life, but that doesn't mean that you'll always be sad when you do. My sadness is not nearly as intense as it was in the beginning, but my love for Eric will never diminish. Eventually your sadness will fade, but your love for your child will endure forever.

EPILOGUE

Eric kept a journal. A few months after he died, I decided to take a quick look at his last entries. Before opening it, I decided that if I saw any intimate thoughts that might embarrass him or me, I'd close it and never look again.

But instead, I discovered that his writings were very inspirational. He used his journal to push himself to be the best he could be. He challenged himself and he set goals for himself.

And when he found something that inspired him, he grabbed a pen and wrote it in his journal.

Eric also loved books. He was always in the middle of a book or two with a couple more ready to go. Shortly before he died, he read *Tuesdays With Morrie* by Mitch Albom. One passage in the book resonated strongly with Eric, so strongly that he stopped to write it in his journal.

When I discovered this, I was stunned. Why this passage meant so much to young, vibrant, 26 year old Eric, I'll never know. But to see these words in his handwriting was amazing. I found this very comforting. And I hope you do too.

From Morrie as told to Mitch as written by Eric:

As long as we love each other and remember the feeling of love we had, we can die without ever really going away. All the love you created is still there. All the memories are still there. You live on – in the hearts of everyone you have touched and nurtured while you were here.

Death ends a life. Not a relationship

ACKNOWLEDGEMENTS

I want to express my appreciation to the people who have helped me throughout the process of writing this book:

Rhonda Robins, Lisa Cox and Melinda Facelli all provided valuable contributions during the editing process. Their observations and suggestions were right every time.

A lot of people have helped me through my grieving and their ongoing support means the world to me. The book would be twice as long if I tried to mention them all by name, but I do want to express special appreciation to Stacey Seidman, Scott Tansey, Cheryl Harding, and Susan Giannotti for checking in on me again and again, and being with me no matter what. I suspect they'll all be surprised that I mentioned them here. I'm sure they felt they were just doing what anyone would do. But for me, their support has been above and beyond.

Rachel Seidman and Julie Johnson suddenly lost a big part of their worlds with Eric's passing. Their grace in the days and months that followed, under impossible circumstances, was and continues to be, a huge inspiration for me.

And finally, I am so fortunate to have Mary Seidman at my side throughout this ordeal. No mom should have to endure what Mary has been through, but she has been there for me every single time I needed her to be as we continue to work our way across the Grand Canyon of our loss.

CONTACT INFO

If you're a dad who has lost a child, you have my deepest sympathy. I know how hard it is.

If you want to reach out to me for any reason, you can do so at this email address: GrievingDadContact@gmail.com.

Please bear in mind that I am not a therapist, but if you just want to talk about it with someone who been through it, send me an email and I'll get back to you as soon as I can.

9 781540 879530